100

SIMPLE WAYS

TO IMPROVE YOUR

PRODUCTIVITY

Productivity is an essential aspect of achieving success in any aspect of life.

Whether it's work, personal goals, or daily tasks, being productive helps you make the most of your time and achieve your goals efficiently.

But sometimes, it's hard to stay focused and motivated. This ebook aims to provide you with 100 simple ways to improve productivity and help you stay on track.

1. Use a planner or calendar to keep track of your tasks and appointments.

Using a planner or calendar to keep track of your tasks and appointments can significantly improve your productivity. Here are some reasons why:

- Helps you prioritize: When you have a planner or calendar, you can see all your tasks and appointments at a glance. This helps you prioritize your tasks and focus on the most important ones first.

- Reduces stress: When you know what you need to do and when you need to do it, you'll feel less stressed and more in control. This can help you stay focused and motivated throughout the day.

- Improves time management: By scheduling your tasks and appointments in advance, you can better manage your time and avoid overloading your schedule. This can help you be more efficient and get more done in less time.

- Helps you remember important deadlines: With a planner or calendar, you can set reminders for important deadlines and appointments. This can help you stay on top of your responsibilities and avoid missing deadlines.

- Provides a sense of accomplishment: Checking off completed tasks in your planner or calendar can give you a sense of accomplishment and motivation to continue being productive.

Overall, using a planner or calendar can help you stay organized, reduce stress, manage your time better, and achieve your goals more efficiently.

2. Create a daily to-do list to prioritize tasks.

Creating a daily to-do list can be a simple yet powerful tool to improve your productivity. Here are some reasons why:

- Provides focus: When you have a to-do list, you know exactly what tasks you need to accomplish each day. This helps you stay focused and avoid getting distracted by other tasks or interruptions.

- Helps you prioritize: By creating a to-do list, you can prioritize your tasks based on their importance and urgency. This helps you focus on the most important tasks first, ensuring that you're making the most of your time and energy.

- Increases efficiency: With a to-do list, you can work more efficiently by avoiding time-wasting activities and focusing on the tasks that matter. This can help you get more done in less time and with less stress.

- Reduces stress: When you have a clear idea of what you need to do each day, you'll feel less stressed and more in control. This can help you stay motivated and focused throughout the day.

- Provides a sense of accomplishment: Checking off completed tasks on your to-do list can give you a sense of accomplishment and progress towards your goals.

Overall, creating a daily to-do list can be a great way to improve your productivity and stay focused on your goals. By prioritizing tasks, increasing efficiency, and reducing stress, you can make the most of your time and achieve more each day.

3. Use time-blocking to schedule your day.

Using time-blocking to schedule your day can be a highly effective technique to improve your productivity. Here are some reasons why:

- Helps you stay organized: When you use time-blocking, you can allocate specific time slots to each task on your to-do list. This helps you stay organized and ensures that you're using your time effectively.

- Increases focus: By dedicating a specific time slot to each task, you can stay focused on that task without getting distracted by other activities. This can help you work more efficiently and get more done in less time.

- Reduces stress: When you have a clear idea of what you need to do and when you need to do it, you'll feel less stressed and more in control. This can help you stay motivated and focused throughout the day.

- Helps you prioritize: Time-blocking can also help you prioritize your tasks by allocating more time to the most important tasks and less time to less important tasks. This ensures that you're focusing on the tasks that matter most, making the most of your time and energy.

- Improves time management: By scheduling your day with time-blocking, you can better manage your time and avoid overloading your schedule. This can help you be more efficient and get more done in less time.

Overall, using time-blocking to schedule your day can be an excellent way to improve your productivity. By staying organized, increasing focus, reducing stress, prioritizing tasks, and managing your time more effectively, you can achieve your goals more efficiently and make the most of your day.

4. Focus on one task at a time.

Focusing on one task at a time can be a powerful way to improve your productivity. Here are some reasons why:

- Increases focus: By focusing on one task at a time, you can give it your full attention without getting distracted by other tasks or interruptions. This can help you work more efficiently and get more done in less time.

- Improves quality: When you focus on one task at a time, you can devote your full attention to it, ensuring that you're doing it to the best of your ability. This can lead to higher quality work and better results.

- Reduces stress: When you have too many tasks on your plate, it can be overwhelming and stressful. By focusing on one task at a time, you can reduce that feeling of overwhelm and feel more in control.

- Increases productivity: Focusing on one task at a time can also help you be more productive overall. By completing tasks more efficiently and to a higher standard, you can accomplish more in less time.

- Helps you prioritize: Focusing on one task at a time can also help you prioritize your tasks. By working on the most important task first, you can ensure that you're making the most of your time and energy.

Overall, focusing on one task at a time can be an effective way to improve your productivity and achieve better results. By increasing focus, improving quality, reducing stress, increasing productivity, and prioritizing tasks, you can make the most of your time and achieve your goals more efficiently.

5. Set deadlines for yourself.

Setting deadlines for yourself can be an effective way to improve your productivity. Here are some reasons why:

- Provides motivation: When you set deadlines for yourself, you create a sense of urgency that can motivate you to work more efficiently and get things done.

- Helps you prioritize: Deadlines can also help you prioritize your tasks by ensuring that you focus on the most important tasks first. This can help you be more productive and make the most of your time.

- Increases accountability: By setting deadlines for yourself, you hold yourself accountable for completing tasks on time. This can help you stay on track and avoid procrastination.

- Reduces stress: When you have a deadline, you know exactly when you need to complete a task, which can help reduce stress and increase your sense of control.

- Improves time management: Setting deadlines can help you better manage your time by ensuring that you allocate enough time for each task. This can help you avoid overcommitting and ensure that you're making the most of your time.

Overall, setting deadlines for yourself can be a useful tool for improving your productivity. By providing motivation, helping you prioritize, increasing accountability, reducing stress, and improving time management, you can achieve your goals more efficiently and make the most of your time.

6. Avoid multitasking.

Avoiding multitasking can be a powerful way to improve your productivity. Here are some reasons why:

● Increases focus: When you avoid multitasking, you can give your full attention to one task at a time, allowing you to complete it more efficiently and with better quality.

● Reduces errors: When you try to do multiple tasks at once, you increase the likelihood of making mistakes. By focusing on one task at a time, you can reduce errors and improve the quality of your work.

● Increases productivity: Multitasking can actually decrease your productivity because it takes time to switch between tasks. By focusing on one task at a time, you can complete it more quickly and move on to the next task more efficiently.

● Reduces stress: Multitasking can be stressful and overwhelming because you're trying to juggle multiple tasks at once. By focusing on one task at a time, you can reduce that feeling of overwhelm and feel more in control.

● Helps you prioritize: When you avoid multitasking, you can better prioritize your tasks by focusing on the most important ones first. This can help you be more productive and make the most of your time.

Overall, avoiding multitasking can be an effective way to improve your productivity and achieve better results. By increasing focus, reducing errors, increasing productivity, reducing stress, and helping you prioritize, you can make the most of your time and achieve your goals more efficiently.

7. Learn to say no to non-essential tasks.

Learning to say no to non-essential tasks can be an important step in improving your productivity. Here are some reasons why:

● Saves time: By saying no to non-essential tasks, you can free up time to focus on the tasks that are most important and valuable. This can help you be more productive and make the most of your time.

● Reduces stress: Saying yes to too many tasks can be overwhelming and stressful. By learning to say no, you can reduce that feeling of overwhelm and feel more in control of your workload.

● Increases focus: When you say no to non-essential tasks, you can better focus on the tasks that are most important and valuable. This can help you be more efficient and effective in completing those tasks.

● Helps you prioritize: By saying no to non-essential tasks, you can better prioritize your workload and focus on the tasks that will have the most impact on your goals.

● Improves work-life balance: Saying no to non-essential tasks can also help you achieve a better work-life balance. By reducing your workload, you can free up time for the things that are important to you outside of work.

Overall, learning to say no to non-essential tasks can be an effective way to improve your productivity and achieve better results. By saving time, reducing stress, increasing focus, helping you prioritize, and improving work-life balance, you can make the most of your time and achieve your goals more efficiently.

8. Break down large tasks into smaller, manageable tasks.

Breaking down large tasks into smaller, manageable tasks can be a helpful technique for improving your productivity. Here are some reasons why:

● Increases motivation: Large tasks can be daunting, which can decrease your motivation to get started. By breaking them down into smaller, more manageable tasks, you can increase your motivation by giving yourself a clear and achievable path forward.

● Reduces overwhelm: Large tasks can also be overwhelming, which can make it difficult to focus and be productive. By breaking them down into smaller tasks, you can reduce that feeling of overwhelm and make the task feel more manageable.

● Improves focus: Breaking down tasks into smaller parts can help you better focus on each individual task, which can increase your efficiency and productivity.

● Helps you prioritize: By breaking down large tasks into smaller tasks, you can better prioritize your workload and focus on the most important tasks first.

● Provides a sense of progress: Completing smaller tasks can give you a sense of progress and achievement, which can increase your motivation and momentum as you work towards completing the larger task.

Overall, breaking down large tasks into smaller, manageable tasks can be an effective way to improve your productivity and achieve better results. By increasing motivation, reducing overwhelm, improving focus, helping you prioritize, and providing a sense of progress, you can make the most of your time and achieve your goals more efficiently.

9. Use timers to stay focused on tasks.

Using timers to stay focused on tasks can be a helpful technique for improving your productivity. Here are some reasons why:

• Increases focus: Timers can help you focus on a specific task for a set period of time, which can increase your efficiency and productivity by reducing distractions and interruptions.

• Provides structure: Timers can provide structure to your workday by breaking it up into manageable chunks of time. This can help you better manage your workload and avoid feeling overwhelmed.

• Helps you prioritize: By setting a timer for each task, you can better prioritize your workload and focus on the most important tasks first.

• Increases motivation: Timers can also increase your motivation by providing a sense of urgency and helping you stay on track with your tasks.

• Improves time management: Using timers can help you better manage your time by giving you a clear idea of how long each task takes and allowing you to schedule your day more effectively.

Overall, using timers to stay focused on tasks can be an effective way to improve your productivity and achieve better results. By increasing focus, providing structure, helping you prioritize, increasing motivation, and improving time management, you can make the most of your time and achieve your goals more efficiently.

10. Take breaks to avoid burnout.

Taking breaks to avoid burnout is a crucial aspect of improving your productivity. Here are some reasons why:

• Increases productivity: Taking regular breaks can help you avoid burnout and recharge your energy levels, which can increase your productivity and help you stay focused throughout the day.

• Reduces stress: Working for long periods without taking breaks can lead to increased stress levels, which can negatively impact your overall wellbeing. Taking breaks can help you reduce stress and maintain a healthier work-life balance.

• Improves creativity: Breaks can provide you with the space and time you need to reflect and generate new ideas. By taking a step back from your work, you may be able to approach your tasks with renewed creativity and inspiration.

• Enhances physical health: Sitting for long periods can have negative effects on your physical health. Taking regular breaks can help you get up and move around, stretch, and take care of your body, which can help you feel better and stay healthier.

• Increases focus: Taking breaks can also help you improve your focus by giving your brain time to rest and recharge. This can help you come back to your work with renewed energy and focus.

Overall, taking breaks to avoid burnout is an essential aspect of improving your productivity and achieving your goals. By increasing productivity, reducing stress, improving creativity, enhancing physical health, and increasing focus, taking breaks can help you make the most of your time and achieve your goals more efficiently.

11. Keep your workspace clean and organized.

Keeping your workspace clean and organized can have a significant impact on your productivity. Here are some reasons why:

• Reduces distractions: A cluttered workspace can be distracting and overwhelming, which can negatively impact your focus and productivity. By keeping your workspace clean and organized, you can reduce distractions and create a more conducive environment for work.

- Saves time: When your workspace is organized, you can easily find the tools and materials you need, which can save you time and increase your efficiency.

- Increases motivation: A clean and organized workspace can help you feel more motivated and focused, which can help you stay on track and accomplish your tasks more efficiently.

- Improves health and safety: A clean workspace can also help improve your health and safety. Cluttered and dirty workspaces can lead to increased stress, allergies, and accidents. A clean workspace can help you avoid these issues and maintain a healthier work environment.

- Boosts creativity: An organized workspace can help stimulate creativity and inspiration. When you have a clear and tidy workspace, you can think more clearly and come up with new ideas more easily.

Overall, keeping your workspace clean and organized can have a significant impact on your productivity and wellbeing. By reducing distractions, saving time, increasing motivation, improving health and safety, and boosting creativity, you can make the most of your time and achieve your goals more efficiently.

12. Use labels and folders to categorize files and documents.

Using labels and folders to categorize files and documents is a useful technique for improving your productivity. Here are some reasons why:

- Increases efficiency: When your files and documents are organized with labels and folders, you can easily find what you need and save time. This can help you work more efficiently and accomplish tasks more quickly.

• Reduces stress: When your files and documents are organized, you can reduce the stress and anxiety that comes with trying to find important information. By having a clear and organized system, you can have peace of mind and avoid feeling overwhelmed.

• Improves collaboration: When working with others, using labels and folders can help you easily share and access relevant files and documents. This can make collaborations more efficient and effective.

• Saves space: By organizing files and documents with labels and folders, you can avoid duplicate copies and save space on your computer or other storage devices.

• Improves security: By categorizing and organizing your files and documents, you can improve their security. You can easily identify sensitive information and protect it from unauthorized access.

Overall, using labels and folders to categorize files and documents can improve your productivity, reduce stress, improve collaboration, save space, and improve security. By having an organized system for your files and documents, you can make the most of your time and accomplish your tasks more efficiently.

13. Use a digital filing system to store and access files easily.

Using a digital filing system to store and access files can be a valuable technique for improving your productivity. Here are some reasons why:

• Increases accessibility: With a digital filing system, you can access your files from anywhere with an internet connection, making it easier to work remotely or on-the-go. This can help you work more efficiently and save time.

● Reduces clutter: By using a digital filing system, you can reduce paper clutter in your workspace and avoid losing important documents. This can help you stay organized and improve your focus.

● Improves collaboration: Digital filing systems can facilitate collaboration with team members by allowing easy access to shared files and documents. This can help you work more efficiently and improve your team's productivity.

● Enhances security: Digital filing systems can provide enhanced security features, such as password protection and encryption, to help protect sensitive information. This can provide peace of mind and avoid potential security breaches.

● Saves time: Digital filing systems can save you time by providing search functions and filters that allow you to quickly locate the files and documents you need. This can help you work more efficiently and avoid wasting time searching for information.

Overall, using a digital filing system to store and access files can be a valuable technique for improving your productivity. By increasing accessibility, reducing clutter, improving collaboration, enhancing security, and saving time, you can make the most of your work time and achieve your goals more efficiently.

14. Keep frequently used items within reach.

Keeping frequently used items within reach is a simple but effective technique for improving your productivity. Here are some reasons why:

• Saves time: When frequently used items are within reach, you can quickly and easily access them without having to waste time searching for them. This can help you work more efficiently and accomplish tasks more quickly.

• Reduces distractions: If you have to get up and search for a frequently used item, you may become distracted and lose focus on the task at hand. By keeping items within reach, you can avoid these distractions and stay focused on your work.

• Increases productivity: When you can access frequently used items quickly and easily, you can work more efficiently and be more productive. This can help you accomplish more tasks in less time and improve your overall productivity.

• Improves organization: Keeping frequently used items within reach can also help improve your overall organization. By having a designated place for these items, you can avoid clutter and confusion in your workspace.

• Enhances comfort: By keeping frequently used items within reach, you can also improve your comfort while working. You can avoid strain and discomfort from reaching for items that are too far away.

Overall, keeping frequently used items within reach can be a simple but effective technique for improving your productivity. By saving time, reducing distractions, increasing productivity, improving organization, and enhancing comfort, you can work more efficiently and accomplish your tasks more effectively.

15. Use a task management app to keep track of your tasks.
Using a task management app can be a valuable technique for improving your productivity. Here are some reasons why:

• Centralizes tasks: A task management app allows you to keep all your tasks in one place, making it easier to stay organized and keep track of your to-do list. This can help you work more efficiently and avoid missing important deadlines.

• Prioritizes tasks: Many task management apps allow you to prioritize your tasks based on their level of importance or urgency. This can help you stay focused on the most important tasks and avoid getting sidetracked by less important ones.

• Sets reminders: Task management apps often have reminder features that can help you stay on track with your tasks. You can set reminders for upcoming deadlines or for tasks that need to be completed at a specific time, helping you avoid missing important deadlines.

• Collaborates with others: Some task management apps allow you to collaborate with others, such as team members or coworkers. This can help you work more efficiently as a team and avoid duplicating efforts.

• Analyzes productivity: Many task management apps offer productivity analytics, which can help you identify areas where you could improve your productivity. You can use this information to make changes to your workflow and improve your overall efficiency.

Overall, using a task management app to keep track of your tasks can be a valuable technique for improving your productivity. By centralizing tasks, prioritizing tasks, setting reminders, collaborating with others, and analysing productivity, you can work more efficiently and achieve your goals more effectively.

16. Use a password manager to keep track of login information.
Using a password manager can be an effective technique for improving your productivity and security online. Here are some reasons why:

- Saves time: A password manager allows you to store all your login information in one secure location. This can save you time by eliminating the need to remember or look up passwords for different accounts.

- Improves security: Password managers generate and store strong passwords, reducing the risk of your accounts being compromised by hackers. This can help you protect sensitive information and avoid potential security breaches.

- Simplifies login process: With a password manager, you can easily and quickly login to your accounts without having to remember or type in login information. This can help you work more efficiently and avoid frustration.

- Syncs across devices: Many password managers offer syncing across devices, allowing you to access your login information from anywhere. This can be especially helpful if you use multiple devices throughout the day.

- Streamlines account creation: Many password managers can also help you create new accounts more quickly by automatically generating strong passwords and filling in login information for you.

Overall, using a password manager to keep track of login information can be a valuable technique for improving your productivity and security online. By saving time, improving security, simplifying the login process, syncing across devices, and streamlining account creation, you can work more efficiently and protect your sensitive information.

17. Use a note-taking app to capture ideas and thoughts.

Using a note-taking app can be a valuable technique for improving your productivity and creativity. Here are some reasons why:

- Captures ideas and thoughts: A note-taking app allows you to capture and organize ideas and thoughts quickly and easily, without the need for pen and paper. This can help you remember important ideas and stay organized.

- Synchronizes across devices: Many note-taking apps offer synchronization across devices, allowing you to access your notes from anywhere. This can be especially helpful if you work from multiple devices throughout the day.

- Organizes notes: Note-taking apps often have organizational features, such as folders, tags, and search functions. This can help you find the notes you need quickly and efficiently.

- Collaborates with others: Some note-taking apps allow you to collaborate with others, such as team members or coworkers. This can be helpful for brainstorming and sharing ideas.

- Integrates with other apps: Many note-taking apps integrate with other apps and services, such as calendars, task managers, and email clients. This can help you streamline your workflow and work more efficiently.

Overall, using a note-taking app to capture ideas and thoughts can be a valuable technique for improving your productivity and creativity. By capturing ideas and thoughts, synchronizing across devices, organizing notes, collaborating with others, and integrating with other apps, you can work more efficiently and effectively.

18. Create a system for keeping track of expenses.

Creating a system for keeping track of expenses can be an effective technique for improving your financial organization and productivity. Here are some reasons why:

• Helps you stay on budget: By keeping track of your expenses, you can better understand your spending habits and create a budget that works for you. This can help you stay on track financially and avoid overspending.

• Makes tax preparation easier: Keeping track of expenses can make it easier to prepare for tax season. By organizing your expenses, you can identify deductions and write-offs that can save you money on taxes.

• Reduces stress: Financial organization can reduce stress and anxiety associated with money management. By keeping track of expenses, you can have a better sense of your financial situation and feel more in control of your finances.

• Saves time: By creating a system for keeping track of expenses, you can save time when it comes to organizing and filing receipts, bills, and other financial documents.

• Helps you make informed decisions: By having a clear picture of your expenses, you can make more informed decisions about your finances. For example, you may be able to identify areas where you can cut back on spending or invest more money for the future.

Overall, creating a system for keeping track of expenses can be a valuable technique for improving your financial organization and productivity. By helping you stay on budget, making tax preparation easier, reducing stress, saving time, and helping you make informed decisions, you can achieve greater financial stability and peace of mind.

19. Create a schedule for routine tasks.

Creating a schedule for routine tasks can be a useful technique for improving your productivity and time management. Here are some reasons why:

- Increases efficiency: By scheduling routine tasks, you can ensure that you're using your time effectively and efficiently. This can help you complete tasks more quickly and free up time for other activities.

- Helps you stay organized: A schedule can help you stay organized and focused on the tasks at hand. By knowing what you need to do and when, you can avoid feeling overwhelmed and reduce the likelihood of forgetting important tasks.

- Reduces decision fatigue: When you create a schedule for routine tasks, you don't have to spend time deciding what to do next. This can reduce decision fatigue and help you conserve mental energy.

- Provides a sense of accomplishment: Crossing tasks off your schedule can provide a sense of accomplishment and motivation to keep going. This can help you stay motivated and productive throughout the day.

- Makes it easier to prioritize: When you have a schedule for routine tasks, it's easier to prioritize your time and focus on the most important tasks. This can help you make progress on important projects and avoid getting sidetracked by less important tasks.

Overall, creating a schedule for routine tasks can be a valuable technique for improving your productivity and time management. By increasing efficiency, helping you stay organized, reducing decision fatigue, providing a sense of accomplishment, and making it easier to prioritize, you can work more effectively and accomplish more each day.

20. Eliminate clutter to reduce distractions.

Eliminating clutter can be a helpful technique for reducing distractions and improving your productivity. Here are some reasons why:

• Reduces visual distractions: When your workspace is cluttered, it can be difficult to focus on your tasks because there are visual distractions everywhere. By eliminating clutter, you can create a more visually calming workspace that allows you to focus better.

• Reduces mental distractions: When you have a cluttered workspace, it can be mentally distracting as well. Your brain may feel overwhelmed and unable to focus on the task at hand. By eliminating clutter, you can reduce mental distractions and increase your focus.

• Saves time: When your workspace is cluttered, it can take longer to find the things you need. By eliminating clutter and organizing your space, you can save time and be more efficient.

• Boosts motivation: A cluttered workspace can be demotivating and make it difficult to get started on tasks. By eliminating clutter, you can create a more inspiring and motivating workspace that encourages productivity.

- Improves health: Cluttered workspaces can also have negative impacts on your physical health. Dust, allergens, and other irritants can accumulate in cluttered spaces, leading to health problems. By eliminating clutter and keeping your workspace clean, you can improve your overall health and well-being.

Overall, eliminating clutter can be a valuable technique for reducing distractions and improving your productivity. By reducing visual and mental distractions, saving time, boosting motivation, and improving your health, you can create a more productive and enjoyable workspace.

21. Create a morning routine to start your day off on the right foot.

Creating a morning routine can be a helpful technique for starting your day off on the right foot and improving your productivity. Here are some reasons why:

- Establishes structure: A morning routine can establish structure and provide a sense of order to your day. When you have a routine, you know what to expect and can start your day with purpose and focus.

- Sets a positive tone: A morning routine can help set a positive tone for the rest of the day. By engaging in activities that make you feel good and energized, you can start the day feeling more positive and motivated.

- Reduces decision fatigue: When you have a morning routine, you don't have to spend time making decisions about what to do first thing in the morning. This can help you conserve mental energy and reduce decision fatigue throughout the day.

● Improves productivity: A morning routine can help you feel more focused and productive throughout the day. By starting the day with intention and purpose, you're more likely to carry that energy with you throughout the day.

● Provides self-care: A morning routine can also provide a space for self-care activities such as exercise, meditation, or journaling. By taking care of yourself first thing in the morning, you can set a positive tone for the day and improve your overall well-being.

Overall, creating a morning routine can be a valuable technique for starting your day off on the right foot and improving your productivity. By establishing structure, setting a positive tone, reducing decision fatigue, improving productivity, and providing self-care, you can create a more enjoyable and productive start to your day.

22. Practice mindfulness to reduce stress and improve focus.

Practising mindfulness can be a helpful technique for reducing stress and improving focus, which can in turn improve your productivity. Here are some reasons why:

● Reduces stress: Mindfulness techniques such as meditation and deep breathing can help reduce stress and anxiety by calming the mind and body. By reducing stress, you can improve your ability to focus and be more productive.

● Improves focus: Mindfulness techniques can also improve your ability to focus by training the mind to stay present and not get distracted by external stimuli. By improving your focus, you can complete tasks more efficiently and effectively.

● Increases self-awareness: Mindfulness practices can increase your self-awareness by helping you become more in tune with your thoughts and emotions. By being more aware of your mental and emotional states, you can better manage stress and improve your ability to focus.

● Boosts creativity: Mindfulness practices can also boost creativity by promoting a state of relaxed alertness that allows new ideas to flow more freely.

● Improves overall well-being: In addition to improving focus and productivity, mindfulness practices can improve overall well-being by reducing stress, improving sleep, and promoting a sense of inner calm and balance.

Overall, practising mindfulness can be a valuable technique for reducing stress and improving focus, which can in turn improve your productivity. By reducing stress, improving focus, increasing self-awareness, boosting creativity, and improving overall well-being, you can enhance your ability to perform at your best both personally and professionally.

23. Set realistic goals for yourself.

Setting realistic goals is an important aspect of improving productivity. Here are some reasons why:

● Provides direction: Setting goals helps to provide direction and focus, giving you a clear idea of what you want to achieve and how you plan to achieve it. This can help you stay motivated and on track, and avoid getting sidetracked by unimportant tasks.

● Creates a sense of accomplishment: Achieving a goal provides a sense of accomplishment and can boost self-confidence, which can motivate you to set and achieve more goals.

● Helps to prioritize tasks: Setting goals helps to prioritize tasks by identifying which tasks are most important and need to be completed first. This can help you manage your time more effectively and avoid wasting time on less important tasks.

● Provides a roadmap: Goals provide a roadmap for achieving success, helping you to break down larger projects into smaller, more manageable steps. This can help you stay organized and focused on the task at hand.

● Enhances productivity: By providing direction, motivation, focus, and organization, setting realistic goals can enhance your productivity and help you achieve success more efficiently.

When setting goals, it's important to make sure they are realistic and achievable. Setting goals that are too ambitious or unrealistic can lead to frustration and demotivation, while setting goals that are too easy can lead to complacency. By setting realistic goals that challenge you without overwhelming you, you can improve your productivity and achieve success in both your personal and professional life.

24. Celebrate your accomplishments, no matter how small.

Celebrating your accomplishments, no matter how small, is an important part of staying motivated and improving productivity. Here are some reasons why:

● Boosts motivation: Celebrating your accomplishments can give you a sense of pride and accomplishment, which can boost your motivation and make you more likely to continue working towards your goals.

● Provides positive reinforcement: Celebrating your accomplishments provides positive reinforcement for your efforts, making you more likely to repeat the behavior that led to the accomplishment.

● Reduces stress: Celebrating your accomplishments can help to reduce stress by reminding you of the progress you have made and the successes you have achieved.

● Enhances self-esteem: Celebrating your accomplishments can enhance your self-esteem and confidence, making you more likely to take on new challenges and achieve even more.

● Improves relationships: Celebrating your accomplishments can also help to strengthen relationships by allowing you to share your successes with others and receive support and encouragement.

It's important to celebrate all of your accomplishments, no matter how small. This can include completing a task on your to-do list, hitting a milestone in a project, or even just getting through a difficult day. Celebrating your accomplishments can be as simple as taking a moment to reflect on your success, treating yourself to something you enjoy, or sharing your accomplishment with others. By celebrating your accomplishments, you can stay motivated, reduce stress, and continue to improve your productivity.

25. Focus on progress, not perfection.

Focusing on progress rather than perfection can help improve productivity in several ways:

● Reduces stress: Focusing on perfection can create a lot of stress and pressure, as you may feel like you need to meet extremely high standards. Focusing on progress instead allows you to celebrate the small wins and milestones along the way, which can help reduce stress and promote a more positive mindset.

● Increases motivation: When you focus on progress, you're more likely to stay motivated because you can see the progress you're making. This can help you stay focused and motivated, even when you encounter setbacks or obstacles.

● Encourages learning: Focusing on progress means that you're more likely to be open to learning from mistakes and failures. You can use those experiences as opportunities to learn and grow, rather than feeling discouraged or giving up.

● Promotes action: When you focus on progress, you're more likely to take action, because you're not paralyzed by the fear of not being perfect. This can help you make progress towards your goals, even if it's not perfect.

● Improves productivity: Focusing on progress can help improve productivity by encouraging you to take action, stay motivated, and learn from your experiences. You're more likely to make progress towards your goals when you focus on progress rather than perfection.

Remember, no one is perfect, and striving for perfection can be an impossible goal. By focusing on progress instead, you can set more realistic goals and make continuous progress towards achieving them. Celebrate the progress you make, no matter how small, and use that momentum to keep moving forward towards your goals.

26. Surround yourself with supportive people.

Surrounding yourself with supportive people can have a positive impact on your productivity in several ways:

• Encouragement and motivation: Supportive people can provide encouragement and motivation when you're feeling stuck or discouraged. They can help you stay focused on your goals and provide you with the support and motivation you need to keep going.

• Accountability: When you have supportive people around you, you're more likely to be held accountable for your actions. This can help you stay on track and make progress towards your goals.

• Positive energy: Supportive people can bring positive energy into your life, which can help improve your mood and overall outlook. This can lead to greater productivity and a more positive mindset.

• Networking: Surrounding yourself with supportive people can also help you expand your network and make new connections. This can lead to new opportunities and ideas that can further improve your productivity and success.

• Learning from others: Supportive people can also provide you with opportunities to learn from their experiences and insights. This can help you gain new perspectives and approaches that can improve your productivity and effectiveness.

Overall, surrounding yourself with supportive people can help improve your productivity and overall well-being. Seek out people who encourage and support you in your goals and aspirations, and be sure to provide support and encouragement to them in return.

27. Take care of your physical health.

Taking care of your physical health is an essential aspect of improving your productivity. Here are some reasons why:

• Energy levels: When you prioritize your physical health by getting enough sleep, eating a healthy diet, and exercising regularly, you'll have more energy to tackle your tasks and stay focused throughout the day.

• Mental clarity: Regular exercise and a healthy diet can help improve your cognitive function, including your memory, attention, and focus. This can help you be more productive and effective in your work.

• Stress reduction: Exercise and other physical activities are great stress relievers. When you manage stress effectively, you'll be better able to stay focused and productive.

• Immune system: Taking care of your physical health can also improve your immune system, making it easier for you to fight off illnesses and avoid missing work due to sickness.

• Better sleep: Good sleep is essential for optimal productivity. When you prioritize your physical health, you'll be more likely to get the quality sleep you need to be at your best.

Overall, taking care of your physical health is a crucial part of being productive. Prioritize healthy habits like regular exercise, a balanced diet, and sufficient sleep to improve your energy, focus, and overall well-being.

28. Get enough sleep.

Getting enough sleep is crucial for productivity. Here are some reasons why:

● Restores energy: Sleep is a time when your body restores energy and repairs itself. When you get enough sleep, you'll have more energy to tackle your tasks and be productive throughout the day.

● Improves cognitive function: Good sleep is important for cognitive function, including memory, attention, and focus. When you get enough sleep, you'll be better able to stay focused and productive.

● Reduces stress: Lack of sleep can contribute to stress, which can negatively impact productivity. When you get enough sleep, you'll be better equipped to manage stress and be more productive.

● Boosts creativity: Good sleep can also boost creativity, which can lead to more innovative and productive work.

● Improves physical health: Lack of sleep is associated with a range of physical health problems, including obesity, diabetes, and heart disease. By getting enough sleep, you can improve your physical health and reduce the risk of these conditions.

In general, adults need 7–9 hours of sleep per night. Prioritizing sleep and establishing good sleep habits can help you be more productive and effective in your work.

29. Take breaks to recharge your batteries.

Taking breaks is essential to maintaining productivity and avoiding burnout. Here are some reasons why:

● Prevents fatigue: Taking breaks can help prevent fatigue, which can negatively impact productivity. Short breaks can help you recharge your batteries and be more focused and productive when you return to your work.

- Boosts creativity: Taking breaks can also boost creativity and help you come up with new ideas. When you take a break, you give your brain a chance to rest and recharge, which can lead to more innovative and productive work.

- Reduces stress: Taking breaks can help reduce stress and prevent burnout. When you take a break, you give yourself a chance to relax and recharge, which can help you manage stress more effectively.

- Improves physical health: Taking breaks can also improve your physical health. Sitting for long periods of time can be detrimental to your health, and taking breaks can help you get up and move around, improving circulation and reducing the risk of health problems associated with a sedentary lifestyle.

In general, it's recommended to take short breaks every 60–90 minutes to maintain productivity and avoid burnout. During your break, try to engage in activities that help you relax and recharge, such as taking a walk, doing some stretching, or listening to music.

30. Practice gratitude to improve your mindset.

Practising gratitude can be a powerful tool to improve your mindset and overall well-being. Here are some reasons why:

- Increases happiness: Gratitude is linked to increased levels of happiness and well-being. When you focus on the good things in your life, you're more likely to feel happy and content.

- Reduces negative thinking: Gratitude can help reduce negative thinking and promote a more positive outlook on life. By focusing on what you're grateful for, you're less likely to dwell on negative thoughts and emotions.

- Improves relationships: Expressing gratitude can help improve your relationships with others. When you show gratitude to others, you're more likely to build stronger connections and foster positive feelings.

- Enhances resilience: Practising gratitude can also help enhance your resilience and ability to cope with challenges. By focusing on what you're grateful for, you can gain perspective and feel more equipped to handle difficult situations.

To practice gratitude, try taking a few moments each day to reflect on the things in your life that you're grateful for. You can write them down in a journal, share them with others, or simply take a moment to think about them. By incorporating gratitude into your daily routine, you can improve your mindset and overall well-being.

31. Use clear and concise language when communicating.

Using clear and concise language when communicating is important for several reasons:

- Helps avoid misunderstandings: Clear and concise language helps ensure that your message is accurately understood by the person or people you're communicating with. This can help prevent misunderstandings and ensure that everyone is on the same page.

- Saves time: When you use clear and concise language, you're able to convey your message more quickly and efficiently. This can save time in both personal and professional settings.

- Builds trust: When you communicate clearly and directly, you're more likely to be seen as trustworthy and reliable. This can help build stronger relationships with others and enhance your professional reputation.

● Demonstrates professionalism: Using clear and concise language is a hallmark of professionalism. It shows that you take your communication seriously and that you respect the time and attention of your audience.

To use clear and concise language when communicating, focus on using simple, straightforward language that gets straight to the point. Avoid using jargon, complex sentences, or overly formal language that can confuse or distract from your message. Take the time to organize your thoughts before speaking or writing, and be mindful of the audience you're communicating with. By using clear and concise language, you can enhance your communication skills and improve your overall effectiveness in both personal and professional settings.

32. Use active listening to understand others.

Active listening is a key component of effective communication. It involves fully focusing on and comprehending what the other person is saying, without distraction or interruption. Here are some reasons why using active listening can help you better understand others:

● Builds stronger relationships: When you actively listen to someone, you demonstrate that you value and respect their thoughts and feelings. This can help build stronger relationships based on trust and understanding.

● Improves communication: By actively listening, you can more accurately interpret what the other person is saying and respond appropriately. This can help prevent misunderstandings and enhance communication between you and others.

● Shows empathy: Active listening involves not only hearing what someone is saying, but also trying to understand their perspective and feelings. This can help you show empathy and support, even in difficult or emotional situations.

● Enhances problem-solving: By fully understanding the other person's perspective, you can more effectively work together to solve problems or address concerns.

To practice active listening, start by giving the other person your full attention. Avoid distractions like phone notifications or side conversations, and focus on what they're saying. Show that you're engaged by using non-verbal cues like nodding or maintaining eye contact. Ask clarifying questions to ensure you fully understand their message, and try to summarize or restate what they've said in your own words to demonstrate that you're listening and to confirm your understanding. By practising active listening, you can improve your communication skills and build stronger, more meaningful relationships with others.

33. Avoid distractions when communicating.

Avoiding distractions when communicating is an important aspect of effective communication. Here are some tips to avoid distractions:

● Find a quiet place: Choose a place where there are fewer distractions, such as a conference room or a private office. If you're working remotely, make sure to choose a quiet spot where you won't be interrupted.

● Turn off notifications: Silence your phone and computer notifications during important conversations to avoid being distracted by them.

● Avoid multitasking: When you're having a conversation with someone, give them your full attention. Avoid trying to do other tasks simultaneously.

- Practice active listening: Engage with the person you're speaking with by asking questions and clarifying points to ensure you fully understand what they're saying.

- Maintain eye contact: This will help you stay focused on the conversation and avoid distractions.

By avoiding distractions, you'll be able to have more productive and meaningful conversations.

34. Use non-verbal cues to convey your message.

Using non-verbal cues can be an effective way to convey your message and communicate more clearly. Here are some tips for using non-verbal cues:

- Maintain eye contact: Looking directly at the person you're communicating with shows that you're engaged in the conversation and that you're interested in what they're saying.

- Use gestures: Hand gestures can help emphasize your message and make it more engaging for the listener.

- Pay attention to your posture: Standing or sitting up straight can convey confidence and professionalism, while slouching can give the impression that you're disinterested or disengaged.

- Use facial expressions: Smiling, nodding, and other facial expressions can show that you're listening and engaged in the conversation.

- Pay attention to the other person's non-verbal cues: By observing the other person's body language, you can get a better sense of how they're feeling and what they're thinking.

By using non-verbal cues effectively, you can enhance your communication skills and convey your message more clearly and effectively.

35. Use positive language to motivate others.

Using positive language is a powerful tool to motivate and inspire others. By choosing to use words that have a positive connotation, you can create a more optimistic and encouraging environment. This can help to build stronger relationships, increase productivity, and boost morale.

Here are some tips for using positive language to motivate others:

- Use words that focus on possibilities and opportunities, rather than limitations and restrictions.

- Use words that inspire and uplift, rather than criticize or discourage.

- Use words that acknowledge and appreciate the efforts of others, rather than taking their work for granted.

- Use words that encourage creativity and innovation, rather than maintaining the status quo.

- Use words that express optimism and confidence in the future, rather than dwelling on the past or present challenges.

By using positive language, you can help to create a more positive and productive environment, and motivate others to reach their full potential.

36. Give and receive feedback openly.

Giving and receiving feedback openly is essential for personal and professional growth. Feedback provides valuable insights that can help individuals improve their performance and achieve their goals. However, giving and receiving feedback can be challenging, and it is essential to approach it with an open mind and a willingness to learn.

Here are some tips for giving and receiving feedback openly:

- Be specific and objective: When giving feedback, be specific about what you observed and how it impacted the situation. Avoid generalizations or judgments that could be interpreted as personal attacks. Similarly, when receiving feedback, try to listen to the specific feedback being given and focus on the facts rather than becoming defensive.

- Focus on the behaviour, not the person: Feedback should be directed towards the behavior, not the individual. By separating the person from the behavior, it becomes easier to understand and accept the feedback without feeling personally attacked.

- Be timely: Feedback should be given in a timely manner so that the situation is fresh in everyone's mind. Delayed feedback can be less effective and less meaningful.

- Be constructive: When giving feedback, provide constructive suggestions for improvement. This can help the individual to understand how to improve their performance and achieve their goals. Similarly, when receiving feedback, try to focus on constructive suggestions for improvement rather than becoming defensive.

- Be open-minded: When giving and receiving feedback, it is important to approach the conversation with an open mind and a willingness to learn. Feedback is an opportunity to improve, and both parties should be open to hearing and implementing suggestions for improvement.

By giving and receiving feedback openly, individuals can improve their performance and achieve their goals. Feedback is a valuable tool for personal and professional growth, and it is essential to approach it with an open mind and a willingness to learn.

37. Use collaborative tools to work with others.

Collaborative tools such as shared documents, project management software, and communication tools can help improve teamwork and productivity. With shared documents, multiple team members can work on the same document simultaneously, reducing the need for sending multiple versions of the same document back and forth.

Project management software can help teams stay organized by keeping track of tasks, deadlines, and progress. Communication tools like chat apps and video conferencing can make it easier for team members to communicate and collaborate, even if they are working remotely or in different locations. By using these tools, teams can work together more efficiently and effectively, leading to better outcomes.

38. Use video conferencing to stay connected with remote team members.

Video conferencing can be an effective way to stay connected with remote team members. It allows for face-to-face communication, which can help build trust and rapport among team members.

It also allows for real-time collaboration and discussion, which can lead to more productive meetings and decision-making processes. Video conferencing tools such as Zoom, Skype, and Google Meet are widely available and easy to use, making it simple to connect with remote team members regardless of location.

39. Use project management tools to keep track of team progress.

Using project management tools can help you stay organized and keep track of team progress when working on a project. These tools typically include features like task assignment, deadline tracking, progress monitoring, and collaboration capabilities.

By using a project management tool, you can ensure that everyone on the team is aware of their responsibilities and deadlines, as well as monitor progress to identify potential issues before they become problems. Additionally, many project management tools allow for easy communication and collaboration between team members, making it easier to work together towards a common goal.

40. Use project management tools to keep track of team progress.

Project management tools are software applications designed to help teams collaborate, plan, and execute projects. These tools typically provide features such as task assignment, scheduling, progress tracking, and team communication.

Using project management tools can be incredibly helpful for keeping track of team progress. They can help you stay organized and ensure that everyone is on the same page about what needs to be done, who is responsible for each task, and when each task is due. This can be especially important when working on complex projects with multiple stakeholders and team members.

One of the main benefits of using project management tools is that they can help you identify potential roadblocks or bottlenecks in your project timeline. By keeping track of each task's progress and completion, you can quickly spot issues and address them before they become major problems. This can help you stay on track and meet your project deadlines.

Some popular project management tools include Asana, Trello, Jira, and Basecamp. Each of these tools has its own unique features and benefits, so it's important to do your research and choose the one that works best for your team and your specific project. Additionally, many project management tools offer integrations with other apps and software, such as time-tracking and invoicing tools, to help streamline your workflow and improve productivity.

41. Use productivity apps to streamline tasks.

Using productivity apps can help streamline your tasks and improve your efficiency. These apps can automate certain tasks, provide reminders, and help you stay focused on your priorities. Apps can help you keep track of your tasks, set deadlines, and collaborate with others.

Additionally, many apps offer integrations with other tools and services, such as calendars and email, to help you manage your work more efficiently. By using productivity apps, you can reduce the time and effort required to manage your tasks, leaving you more time to focus on the work that matters most.

42. Use automation tools to save time.

Automation tools can be incredibly useful for streamlining repetitive tasks and saving time. They allow you to automate a wide variety of tasks, from scheduling social media posts to sending email responses.

One popular automation tool is Zapier, which allows you to connect different apps and automate tasks between them. For example, you can create a zap that automatically saves email attachments to Google Drive, or one that automatically adds new leads from a form to your CRM.

Another popular automation tool is IFTTT (If This Then That), which allows you to create applets that connect different services and automate tasks between them. For example, you can create an applet that automatically adds a task to your to-do list whenever a new email is received from a specific sender.

Using automation tools can save you a lot of time and help you stay more organized. However, it's important to remember that not every task can be automated, and sometimes it's better to handle certain tasks manually. It's also important to test your automations regularly to ensure they are working properly and to make any necessary adjustments.

43. Use keyboard shortcuts to work faster.

Using keyboard shortcuts is a great way to work more efficiently and save time. Instead of relying on the mouse or touchpad, keyboard shortcuts allow you to perform tasks quickly and easily, without having to navigate menus or click buttons.

Here are some keyboard shortcuts that can help you work faster:

- Copy: Ctrl + C (Windows) or Command + C (Mac)
- Paste: Ctrl + V (Windows) or Command + V (Mac)
- Cut: Ctrl + X (Windows) or Command + X (Mac)
- Undo: Ctrl + Z (Windows) or Command + Z (Mac)
- Redo: Ctrl + Y (Windows) or Command + Shift + Z (Mac)
- Select all: Ctrl + A (Windows) or Command + A (Mac)
- Save: Ctrl + S (Windows) or Command + S (Mac)
- Print: Ctrl + P (Windows) or Command + P (Mac)
- Find: Ctrl + F (Windows) or Command + F (Mac)
- New document: Ctrl + N (Windows) or Command + N (Mac)

These are just a few examples, but most programs have a variety of keyboard shortcuts that can save you time and make your work more efficient.

44. Use voice-to-text software to transcribe notes.

Using voice-to-text software can be a great way to save time and transcribe notes more quickly. There are many different software options available, including built-in voice-to-text features in programs like Google Docs or Microsoft Word, as well as standalone software like Dragon NaturallySpeaking or Otter.ai. With voice-to-text software, you can speak your notes or ideas and the software will transcribe them into text, saving you time and effort. It's important to note that the accuracy of the transcription may vary depending on the software and the clarity of your speech, so it's always a good idea to double-check the text for errors.

45. Use cloud-based storage to access files from anywhere.

Using cloud-based storage is an effective way to store and access files from anywhere with an internet connection. Cloud storage services, such as Google Drive, Dropbox, and OneDrive, offer users a secure way to store and share files online. Benefits of using cloud-based storage include:

- Accessibility: Cloud storage allows you to access your files from anywhere with an internet connection, making it easy to work remotely or collaborate with others.

- Security: Cloud storage providers offer robust security features to protect your files from unauthorized access or theft. This includes encryption, two-factor authentication, and access controls.

- Backup: Cloud storage providers offer automatic backup features, which can help prevent data loss in the event of hardware failure, theft, or other disasters.

- Scalability: Cloud storage providers offer scalable storage options, allowing you to expand your storage as your needs grow.

- Cost-effectiveness: Cloud storage can be a cost-effective solution, as you only pay for the storage space you need, and you don't have to worry about hardware or maintenance costs.

46. Use online tools to collaborate with team members.

There are many online tools available to facilitate collaboration among team members, regardless of their location. These tools allow team members to work together in real-time, share information, and collaborate on projects.

Some popular online collaboration tools include:

- Google Drive: A cloud-based storage and collaboration platform that allows users to create, share, and edit documents, spreadsheets, and presentations in real-time.

● Trello: A project management tool that allows teams to organize tasks and projects on a virtual board. It's great for tracking progress and assigning tasks to team members.

● Slack: A messaging app that allows teams to communicate in real-time. Slack also integrates with many other productivity tools, making it a powerful collaboration tool.

● Asana: A project management tool that allows teams to track tasks and projects, and collaborate on them in real-time. It's great for managing complex projects with multiple team members.

● Zoom: A video conferencing tool that allows teams to meet virtually. Zoom also allows screen sharing and collaboration on documents in real-time.

By using these online tools, teams can work together seamlessly, regardless of their location. This can improve productivity, increase efficiency, and streamline communication.

47. Use a second monitor to increase productivity.

Using a second monitor can be a great way to increase productivity by giving you more screen real estate to work with. With a second monitor, you can have multiple applications open and visible at the same time, allowing you to work more efficiently and switch between tasks more quickly.

For example, you could have your email and calendar open on one monitor while you work on a project on the other. This can help you stay focused on your work while still being able to keep an eye on important notifications.

Additionally, a second monitor can be useful for tasks that require a lot of screen space, such as graphic design or video editing. Having a larger workspace can make it easier to see and manipulate elements, reducing the amount of scrolling or zooming required.

Overall, using a second monitor can be a simple yet effective way to increase your productivity and make your workday more efficient.

48. Use noise-canceling headphones to reduce distractions.

Using noise-canceling headphones can help reduce distractions and improve focus. They work by actively canceling out external noise, allowing you to focus on your work or task at hand. Noise-canceling headphones are especially useful in busy or noisy environments, such as a crowded office or a coffee shop.

They can also be helpful if you need to concentrate on a particular task, such as writing or coding. By reducing outside distractions, noise-canceling headphones can help improve your productivity and make it easier to stay focused.

49. Take breaks to move your body and prevent physical fatigue.

Taking breaks to move your body can help prevent physical fatigue and reduce the risk of developing injuries related to sitting for prolonged periods. When we sit for extended periods, our bodies tend to become stiff and sore, especially in our neck, back, and shoulders. Taking breaks to move around and stretch can help to alleviate these discomforts and prevent them from worsening.

One way to incorporate movement breaks into your workday is to set a timer for 30-60 minutes and take a five-minute break to stretch or move around when the timer goes off. During this break, you can do some light exercises, such as walking around the office, doing some stretches or yoga poses, or even taking a quick walk outside. This can help to increase blood flow to your muscles, reduce muscle tension, and improve your overall physical and mental health.

In addition to taking regular movement breaks, it's important to maintain good posture while you work. You can do this by keeping your feet flat on the ground, your back straight, and your shoulders relaxed. You can also adjust the height of your chair and desk to ensure that your computer screen is at eye level and your keyboard and mouse are within easy reach. This can help to reduce strain on your neck, back, and shoulders, which can lead to chronic pain and discomfort.

Overall, taking regular breaks to move your body is an essential part of staying healthy and productive at work. By incorporating these breaks into your workday, you can reduce physical fatigue, increase your energy levels, and improve your overall well-being.

50. Use a time-tracking app to measure productivity.

Using a time-tracking app can be a valuable tool in measuring productivity. It allows you to track how much time you spend on various tasks throughout the day, and can help you identify areas where you may be spending too much time or areas where you could be more efficient.

With a time-tracking app, you can also set goals for how much time you want to spend on certain tasks, and see how well you are meeting those goals. This can help you stay focused and motivated throughout the day.

Additionally, time-tracking apps can help you identify patterns in your workday, such as when you are most productive or when you tend to experience a slump in energy. Armed with this knowledge, you can adjust your work schedule and habits accordingly to maximize your productivity.

Overall, using a time-tracking app can provide valuable insights into your work habits and help you optimize your productivity.

51. Read books and articles to learn new skills.

Reading books and articles is a great way to continue learning and expanding your knowledge and skills. It allows you to gain new perspectives and ideas, and to stay up-to-date with the latest trends and developments in your industry or field of interest.

To make the most of your reading time, consider setting aside dedicated time each day or week to read, whether it's during your commute, before bed, or on the weekends. Make a list of books and articles that you want to read and prioritize them based on their relevance to your goals and interests.

It's also helpful to take notes or highlight key points as you read, as this can aid in retention and help you better remember the information later on. Finally, don't be afraid to discuss what you've read with others, whether it's with colleagues, friends, or online communities. This can help deepen your understanding and provide new insights and perspectives.

52. Take online courses to improve your knowledge.

Taking online courses is a great way to improve your knowledge and learn new skills. There are many online platforms that offer courses in various subjects, from programming and data analysis to marketing and design.

Some popular online course platforms include Coursera, edX, Udemy, and Skillshare. These platforms offer courses taught by industry experts and are often affordable or even free.

Online courses are a great way to gain new knowledge and skills, improve your resume, and advance your career. They also provide a flexible learning environment, allowing you to learn at your own pace and on your own schedule.

53. Attend conferences and workshops to network and learn.

Attending conferences and workshops can be a great way to network with professionals in your industry and learn new skills or knowledge. By attending these events, you can gain insights into industry trends, best practices, and the latest research. You can also make valuable connections with like-minded individuals and potentially find new job opportunities.

When attending conferences and workshops, it's important to come prepared. Research the event beforehand to get an idea of the topics that will be covered and the speakers who will be presenting. Take notes during the presentations and engage in discussions with other attendees to make the most of the experience.

Additionally, consider volunteering or presenting at these events to increase your visibility and demonstrate your expertise. By taking an active role in the conference or workshop, you can further establish yourself as a thought leader in your field.

54. Use podcasts to learn on-the-go.

Podcasts are a great way to learn and expand your knowledge while on-the-go. They are convenient, portable, and come in a wide range of topics, making it easy to find a show that matches your interests. You can listen to podcasts while commuting, doing household chores, or even during a workout.

To get started, you can search for podcasts on a variety of platforms, such as Apple Podcasts, Spotify, or Google Podcasts. Look for shows that align with your interests or career goals, and subscribe to them for regular updates. Many podcasts also feature expert guests, so you can learn from their insights and experiences.

Some popular podcasts for personal and professional development include "The Tim Ferriss Show," "TED Talks Daily," "The School of Greatness," "HBR IdeaCast," "Entrepreneur on Fire," and "Optimal Living Daily."

55. Join online communities to connect with others.

Joining online communities can be a great way to connect with others who share similar interests or goals. Whether you're interested in personal development, professional growth, or a particular hobby, there are likely online communities that you can join to connect with others who share your passions.

Some benefits of joining online communities include:

- Learning from others: You can learn from others who have more experience or expertise in a particular area.

- Support: You can get support and encouragement from others who understand what you're going through and can offer advice or guidance.

- Networking: You can connect with others who may be able to help you in your personal or professional life.

- Friendship: You can make new friends who share your interests and passions.

When joining an online community, it's important to be respectful of others and to follow any guidelines or rules that the community may have. You can find online communities through social media platforms, forums, and other online groups.

56. Learn from your mistakes and failures.

Learning from your mistakes and failures is an important aspect of personal and professional growth. Rather than dwelling on your mistakes, it's important to reflect on them and identify what went wrong, what you can learn from the experience, and how you can improve for the future.

This mindset can help you become more resilient, adaptable, and confident in your abilities, as you will develop the ability to navigate challenges and setbacks with a more positive and proactive attitude. Remember, failure is not the opposite of success, but rather a part of the journey towards achieving it.

57. Ask for help when you need it.

Asking for help is an important skill that can benefit you both personally and professionally. It's important to recognize when you need help and to seek it out when necessary.

Asking for help can come in many forms, whether it's asking a coworker for clarification on a project, seeking advice from a mentor, or even asking a friend for emotional support. It's important to remember that everyone needs help at some point, and seeking help is not a sign of weakness.

When asking for help, be clear about what you need and why you need it. Be respectful of the other person's time and be willing to reciprocate if they need help in the future. By asking for help, you can gain valuable knowledge, skills, and perspectives that can help you grow and succeed.

58. Share your knowledge with others.

Sharing your knowledge with others is a great way to solidify your own understanding of a subject and to help others learn. Here are some ways you can share your knowledge:

- Write a blog or create a podcast: Sharing your knowledge through blogging or podcasting can help you reach a wider audience and establish yourself as an authority in your field.

- Teach a class: If you're an expert in a particular subject, consider teaching a class or workshop to share your knowledge with others in a more structured setting.

- Volunteer your time: Consider volunteering your time to help others learn. This could involve tutoring students or teaching a class at a community center or library.

- Participate in online communities: Engage in online communities related to your area of expertise and share your knowledge by answering questions or contributing to discussions.

- Mentor others: Consider mentoring someone who is just starting out in your field. This is a great way to share your knowledge and help someone else succeed.

59. Challenge yourself to learn something new every day.

Learning something new every day can help you expand your knowledge and improve your skills. It can also help keep your mind active and engaged. Here are some tips on how to challenge yourself to learn something new every day:

• Set a goal: Make it a goal to learn something new every day. This could be anything from learning a new word to learning a new skill.

• Read: Read books, articles, and other materials to learn about new topics. You can also subscribe to newsletters or blogs that cover topics that interest you.

• Take notes: When you learn something new, take notes on what you learned. This will help you remember the information and reinforce your learning.

• Watch videos: YouTube and other video sharing platforms have a wealth of educational content that you can watch to learn new things.

• Attend workshops or webinars: Look for online workshops or webinars that cover topics that interest you. These can be great opportunities to learn from experts in a particular field.

• Talk to experts: If there's a topic you're interested in, try to find an expert in that field and ask them questions. This can be a great way to learn more about a subject and get personalized advice.

• Learn from your mistakes: When you make a mistake, take the opportunity to learn from it. Reflect on what went wrong and what you can do differently next time.

Remember, learning something new every day doesn't have to be a big undertaking. It can be as simple as learning a new word or trying a new recipe. The important thing is to keep your mind engaged and constantly learning.

60. Set learning goals for yourself.

Setting learning goals for yourself is a great way to stay motivated and focused on your personal and professional development. Here are some tips to help you set effective learning goals:

● Identify your strengths and weaknesses: Take a moment to reflect on your current skills and knowledge. What are you good at? What do you need to improve?

● Determine your learning style: Everyone has a unique learning style. Some people prefer visual learning, while others prefer auditory or kinesthetic learning. Understanding your learning style can help you choose the right learning resources and methods that work best for you.

● Choose a specific learning goal: When setting your learning goals, be specific about what you want to achieve. For example, instead of saying "I want to learn more about marketing," say "I want to learn how to create and implement an effective social media marketing strategy."

● Break down your goal into smaller tasks: Once you have identified your specific learning goal, break it down into smaller tasks that are easier to accomplish. This will help you stay motivated and make progress toward your larger goal.

● Set a timeline: Give yourself a deadline for achieving your learning goal. This will help you stay accountable and focused on your progress.

Remember, learning is a lifelong journey. Setting learning goals for yourself is a great way to stay engaged and motivated as you continue to grow and develop.

61. Wake up early to start your day off right.

Waking up early has numerous benefits, such as having more time in the day to accomplish tasks, better mental clarity and focus, and improved overall productivity. By waking up early, you can establish a routine that allows you to start your day in a calm and organized manner, without feeling rushed or stressed.

One tip for waking up early is to establish a consistent sleep schedule by going to bed and waking up at the same time every day, including weekends. This helps regulate your body's internal clock and makes it easier to wake up in the morning.

Another tip is to create a morning routine that motivates and energizes you. This can include activities like exercise, meditation, reading, or journaling. By starting your day with positive habits, you set the tone for the rest of your day and increase your chances of having a productive and successful day.

62. Exercise regularly to improve your health and mindset.

Regular exercise has numerous benefits for both physical and mental health. Exercise can help to reduce stress, increase energy levels, improve sleep quality, and boost self-esteem. It can also help to prevent chronic health conditions such as heart disease, diabetes, and obesity.

To incorporate exercise into your daily routine, you can start by setting aside time each day for physical activity. This could include going for a walk or jog, taking a yoga or fitness class, or participating in a team sport. It's also important to find a type of exercise that you enjoy, so that it feels more like a rewarding activity than a chore.

Remember to start slowly and gradually increase the intensity and duration of your exercise as your fitness level improves. It's also important to listen to your body and rest when you need to, to avoid injury and burnout. With consistent effort, exercise can become a habit that helps you to feel better and perform at your best.

63. Eat a healthy, balanced diet to fuel your body and mind.

Maintaining a healthy and balanced diet is essential for your physical and mental well-being. Your diet should include a variety of nutrient-dense foods, such as fruits, vegetables, whole grains, lean proteins, and healthy fats. These foods provide your body with the energy and nutrients it needs to function properly.

Eating a balanced diet can also help improve your mood, increase your focus and concentration, and reduce your risk of developing chronic diseases such as obesity, diabetes, and heart disease.

To maintain a healthy and balanced diet, aim to:

- Eat a variety of fruits and vegetables every day

- Choose whole grains instead of refined grains

- Incorporate lean proteins such as chicken, fish, tofu, and legumes

- Limit your intake of saturated and trans fats, and instead, choose healthy fats such as avocado, nuts, and olive oil

- Reduce your intake of added sugars and salt

- Stay hydrated by drinking plenty of water throughout the day.

Remember, it's okay to indulge in your favorite treats from time to time, but overall, aim to make healthy food choices to support your overall health and well-being.

64. Find a form of stress relief that works for you, such as meditation, yoga, or journaling, and make time for it regularly.

Engaging in activities that promote relaxation and reduce stress is crucial for maintaining good mental health and overall wellbeing. Meditation, yoga, and journaling are all effective methods for managing stress, but it's important to find a technique that works best for you.

Meditation involves sitting quietly and focusing on your breath or a specific object, allowing your mind to relax and become more present. Regular meditation has been shown to decrease stress, anxiety, and depression and improve overall mental health.

Yoga is a physical and mental practice that combines movement, breath work, and meditation. It can help reduce stress, increase flexibility, and improve overall physical and mental health.

Journaling involves writing down your thoughts and feelings, which can help you process emotions and manage stress. It can be done in a traditional notebook or digitally through an app.

Finding time for stress-relieving activities can be challenging, but it's important to prioritize your mental health and wellbeing. Even just a few minutes of meditation, yoga, or journaling each day can make a big difference in reducing stress and improving your overall mindset.

65. Practice deep breathing to reduce stress and improve focus.

Deep breathing is a simple yet effective technique to reduce stress and improve focus. It involves taking slow, deep breaths from the diaphragm rather than shallow breaths from the chest.

To practice deep breathing, find a quiet and comfortable place to sit or lie down. Close your eyes and take a deep breath in through your nose, counting to four as you inhale. Hold your breath for a count of four, then exhale slowly through your mouth for a count of four. Repeat this cycle several times, focusing on the rhythm of your breath and letting go of any distracting thoughts.

Deep breathing can be done at any time throughout the day, whether you're feeling stressed or just need a moment to refocus. It's a simple and effective way to calm your mind and body and improve your overall well-being.

66. Meditate to improve mindfulness and clarity of thought.

Meditation is a technique that involves focusing one's attention on a particular object, thought, or activity to achieve a mentally clear and emotionally calm state. Regular meditation practice has been shown to improve mindfulness, reduce stress and anxiety, enhance emotional regulation, and increase cognitive flexibility.

To start a meditation practice, find a quiet and comfortable place where you won't be disturbed. Sit or lie down in a relaxed position and close your eyes. Focus your attention on your breath, observing the sensation of the air moving in and out of your body. Whenever your mind starts to wander, gently bring your attention back to your breath.

Start with just a few minutes of meditation each day and gradually increase the time as you become more comfortable.

There are also many guided meditation apps and resources available that can help you get started with a meditation practice or deepen your existing practice.

67. Avoid procrastination by setting deadlines and sticking to them.

Procrastination is a common problem that can negatively impact productivity and cause stress. One way to avoid procrastination is to set deadlines for yourself and make sure you stick to them. Here are some tips on how to do this:

- Break tasks into smaller parts: When faced with a large project, it can be overwhelming and tempting to procrastinate. Instead, break the project into smaller, more manageable tasks and set deadlines for each one. This can help you focus on one task at a time and make progress without feeling overwhelmed.

- Use a task management app: There are many apps available that can help you keep track of tasks and deadlines. Find one that works for you and use it to set deadlines and track your progress.

- Hold yourself accountable: If you struggle with sticking to deadlines, find someone who can hold you accountable. This could be a coworker, friend, or family member who you trust and who will check in on your progress.

- Create consequences: Another way to hold yourself accountable is to create consequences for missing a deadline. For example, you could donate money to a charity for every day you miss a deadline or give up a favorite activity for a week.

Remember, the key to avoiding procrastination is to take action and set realistic deadlines for yourself. With practice and perseverance, you can improve your productivity and achieve your goals.

68. Learn to prioritize tasks effectively.

- Learning to prioritize tasks effectively is crucial for productivity and time management. Here are some tips:

- Make a to-do list: Write down all the tasks you need to complete and prioritize them based on their importance and urgency.

- Identify deadlines: Determine when each task needs to be completed and prioritize accordingly.

- Break down larger tasks: If a task seems overwhelming, break it down into smaller, manageable steps.

- Evaluate your workload: Take a step back and evaluate the amount of work you have to do. Determine what is most important and focus on that first.

- Use the 80/20 rule: The Pareto Principle suggests that 80% of the results come from 20% of the effort. Identify the 20% of tasks that will yield the most results and prioritize those.

- Delegate tasks: If possible, delegate tasks to others who are better equipped to handle them or have more time available.

- Learn to say no: If a task is not important or urgent, say no or delegate it to someone else.

Remember that effective prioritization is an ongoing process and requires constant evaluation and adjustment.

69. Eliminate distractions by turning off notifications.

One of the most common productivity killers is distractions, especially those coming from notifications on our electronic devices. To eliminate these distractions, a helpful tip is to turn off notifications. This could include notifications for email, social media, messaging apps, and other non-essential applications.

By turning off notifications, you can regain control of your attention and stay focused on your work. You can also set specific times to check your notifications instead of allowing them to interrupt you throughout the day. This simple change can help you accomplish more in less time and reduce stress and anxiety caused by constant interruptions.

70. Use positive affirmations to boost confidence and motivation.

Positive affirmations are a powerful tool that can help you build confidence, motivation, and a positive mindset. They are simple, yet effective statements that you repeat to yourself regularly, either silently or out loud. By doing so, you can begin to reprogram your thoughts and beliefs about yourself and the world around you.

To use positive affirmations, start by identifying the areas in your life where you would like to improve. Then, create a list of affirmations that align with those goals. For example, if you want to improve your self-confidence, you might repeat affirmations like, "I am confident in myself and my abilities," or "I trust myself to make the right decisions."

Once you have your list of affirmations, find a quiet place where you can repeat them to yourself. You might choose to do this in the morning before starting your day, or in the evening before going to bed. Repeat each affirmation several times, focusing on the words and their meaning.

Over time, you may notice that your thoughts and beliefs begin to shift, and you feel more confident, motivated, and positive. It's important to remember that affirmations are just one tool in your personal development toolbox, and they work best when combined with other healthy habits and practices.

71. Create a comfortable work environment to reduce stress.

Creating a comfortable work environment is important to help reduce stress and increase productivity. Here are some tips to achieve this:

- Choose a space that is quiet and free from distractions. This could be a separate room in your home or a designated workspace in a shared area.

- Make sure your workspace is well-lit and has good ventilation. Natural light is ideal, but if this is not possible, invest in a good desk lamp and avoid harsh overhead lighting.

- Invest in comfortable furniture, including a supportive chair and desk at the right height for your needs.

- Keep your workspace organized and tidy. This includes clearing away clutter, keeping important items within easy reach, and using storage solutions such as shelves or filing cabinets.

- Add personal touches that make you feel comfortable and inspired, such as plants, artwork, or photos.

By creating a comfortable and organized workspace, you can help reduce stress and improve your focus and productivity.

72. Use natural light to boost mood and productivity.

Using natural light is a great way to boost mood and productivity in the workplace. Natural light is a free, renewable resource that provides numerous benefits, including better visibility, reduced eye strain, and increased alertness.

To make the most of natural light, consider the following tips:

● Position your desk near a window: If possible, position your desk near a window to allow natural light to flood your workspace. This can help to reduce eye strain and make you feel more alert.

● Adjust your blinds or curtains: If the natural light is too bright or too dim, adjust your blinds or curtains accordingly. You can also use sheer curtains to diffuse the light and create a softer, more natural glow.

● Use mirrors: Mirrors can help to reflect natural light and increase the amount of light in your workspace. Position mirrors strategically around your workspace to make the most of natural light.

● Take breaks outside: Taking regular breaks outside can help to expose you to natural light and improve your mood and productivity.

Overall, using natural light is a simple and effective way to improve your workspace and boost your productivity.

73. Use ergonomic furniture to reduce strain on the body.

Ergonomic furniture is designed to support good posture and reduce strain on the body during long periods of sitting or standing. This type of furniture can help prevent back pain, neck pain, and other musculoskeletal disorders that can result from poor posture or repetitive movements.

When choosing ergonomic furniture, look for chairs and desks that can be adjusted to fit your body and your workspace. This may include features such as adjustable seat height, lumbar support, and armrests on chairs, as well as adjustable desk height, tilt, and monitor height on desks.

Investing in ergonomic furniture can not only help improve your physical health, but also improve your productivity by reducing discomfort and fatigue during long work sessions.

74. Use plants to improve air quality and create a calming atmosphere.

Adding plants to your workspace can offer numerous benefits, including improving air quality, reducing stress, and increasing productivity. Research has shown that being in the presence of plants can help lower blood pressure, reduce anxiety and fatigue, and increase overall feelings of well-being.

Plants also have the ability to purify the air by removing harmful pollutants, such as benzene and formaldehyde, from the air. This can result in improved air quality, which can lead to fewer sick days and better overall health.

In addition to these health benefits, plants can also improve your workspace aesthetically. They can add color, texture, and life to an otherwise sterile environment, creating a more pleasant and inviting atmosphere.

When choosing plants for your workspace, be sure to select ones that are low-maintenance and appropriate for the amount of natural light in your workspace. Good options include succulents, cacti, and spider plants, which require minimal watering and can thrive in a variety of lighting conditions.

75. Use color psychology to create a productive workspace.

Color psychology suggests that colors can impact our mood, emotions, and productivity. When designing a workspace, it's important to choose colors that promote focus, creativity, and relaxation.

For example, blue is often associated with calmness and productivity, while yellow is linked to creativity and energy. Green is thought to reduce eye strain and promote relaxation, making it a good choice for those who spend long hours in front of a computer. Red can be stimulating and energizing, but it can also be overwhelming in large amounts.

Consider using a color scheme that incorporates these colors, as well as other hues that align with the goals of your workspace. Additionally, think about the overall ambiance you want to create and choose colors that contribute to that vibe. For example, if you want to create a calming and serene environment, you may want to incorporate shades of blue and green. If you want to create a more dynamic and stimulating environment, you may want to use brighter and bolder colors.

76. Use aromatherapy to improve focus and reduce stress.

Aromatherapy is a form of alternative medicine that uses essential oils to improve physical and mental well-being. Essential oils are concentrated extracts from plants that are believed to have therapeutic properties. Aromatherapy is often used as a natural way to reduce stress, anxiety, and depression, and to improve focus and concentration.

Some essential oils that are commonly used in aromatherapy for productivity and stress relief include:

- Peppermint: Known for its invigorating and energizing properties, peppermint oil can help improve focus and concentration.

- Lavender: Often used for its calming and relaxing properties, lavender oil can help reduce stress and anxiety.

- Lemon: Known for its uplifting and refreshing scent, lemon oil can help improve mood and energy.

- Rosemary: Believed to enhance memory and cognitive function, rosemary oil can help improve mental clarity and focus.

To use aromatherapy for productivity, you can add a few drops of essential oil to a diffuser or oil burner and inhale the scent. You can also add a drop or two of oil to a tissue or handkerchief and inhale deeply when needed. It's important to note that essential oils can be powerful and should be used with caution. Always dilute essential oils before applying them to the skin, and avoid using them near the eyes or on sensitive skin.

77. Keep the temperature comfortable to improve concentration.

Maintaining a comfortable temperature is important for productivity and concentration. When the temperature is too hot or too cold, it can cause discomfort and distraction, which can lead to decreased work performance. The ideal temperature for a workspace is generally between 68-72°F (20-22°C), but this can vary depending on personal preferences and the type of work being done.

Keeping the workspace well-ventilated and using fans or heaters can also help regulate the temperature and create a more comfortable working environment. It's important to pay attention to your body's signals and adjust the temperature as needed to ensure that you can stay focused and productive throughout the day.

78. Use background noise to improve focus.

Some people find that background noise can help them concentrate and drown out distractions. However, the type of noise that works best can vary from person to person. Some prefer white noise or instrumental music, while others may prefer nature sounds or even ambient noise from a coffee shop or library.

There are many apps and websites available that provide various background noise options. Experiment with different types of noise to find what works best for you.

79. Use natural scents to create a calming environment.

Aromatherapy can be a powerful tool for promoting relaxation and reducing stress. There are a variety of natural scents that can be used to create a calming environment, including lavender, chamomile, jasmine, and ylang-ylang.

Lavender is a popular scent for promoting relaxation and reducing anxiety. It has been shown to lower heart rate and blood pressure, and can improve the quality of sleep.

Chamomile is another scent that is known for its calming properties. It has a sweet, floral aroma that can help to ease tension and promote relaxation.

Jasmine is a soothing scent that can help to reduce anxiety and improve mood. It has been shown to promote relaxation and improve the quality of sleep.

Ylang-ylang is a tropical flower with a sweet, floral scent that can help to reduce stress and promote relaxation. It has been shown to lower blood pressure and heart rate, and can improve mood and overall well-being.

To use natural scents for relaxation, you can use essential oils, candles, or diffusers. Essential oils can be added to a carrier oil and applied to the skin, or added to a bath or shower. Candles can be lit to release the scent into the air, and diffusers can be used to distribute the scent throughout a room.

80. Use feng shui principles to improve energy flow in your workspace.

Feng shui is an ancient Chinese practice that aims to harmonize individuals with their surrounding environment. By incorporating feng shui principles into your workspace, you can enhance the flow of energy and create a more balanced and productive environment. Here are some feng shui tips for your workspace:

- Clear clutter: Clutter can disrupt the flow of energy in your workspace, so it's essential to keep your desk clean and tidy. Get rid of any unnecessary items, and only keep what you need within reach.

• Choose the right colors: Different colors can have a significant impact on your mood and productivity. Choose colors that resonate with you and your work goals. For example, blue is often associated with calmness and productivity, while yellow is said to promote creativity.

• Place your desk in the command position: The command position is the spot in your workspace that gives you the best view of the door. This position is said to promote a sense of security and control, which can boost confidence and productivity.

• Incorporate natural elements: Adding plants, rocks, and other natural elements to your workspace can help bring in positive energy and promote a sense of calm and serenity.

• Consider the lighting: Lighting is essential in creating a comfortable and productive workspace. Natural light is always the best option, but if that's not possible, try to incorporate full-spectrum light bulbs.

By incorporating feng shui principles into your workspace, you can create a more harmonious and productive environment that supports your work goals and enhances your overall well-being.

81. Set personal goals to improve your life.

Setting personal goals can help you achieve your desired outcomes and improve your life. Here are some tips for setting personal goals:

• Make your goals specific and measurable: Set clear goals with specific, measurable outcomes so that you know when you have achieved them.

● Set realistic goals: Make sure your goals are achievable and realistic. Setting unrealistic goals can lead to frustration and disappointment.

● Break down larger goals into smaller, manageable ones: If you have a larger goal, break it down into smaller, manageable goals. This will make it easier to track your progress and keep you motivated.

● Write down your goals: Write down your goals and keep them in a visible place. This will help you stay focused and motivated.

● Review your goals regularly: Review your goals regularly to ensure that you are making progress and staying on track.

Remember, setting personal goals can be a powerful way to improve your life, but it's important to be patient and persistent.

82. Identify your strengths and weaknesses.

Identifying your strengths and weaknesses is an important step towards personal and professional growth. By knowing your strengths, you can capitalize on them to achieve your goals, while being aware of your weaknesses helps you to work on them and improve yourself.

To identify your strengths, consider the things that come naturally to you, the things that you enjoy doing, and the things that you receive praise for. These could be skills, personality traits, or talents.

To identify your weaknesses, think about the areas where you struggle, the things that make you uncomfortable, and the areas where you receive criticism. It is important to be honest with yourself and not be defensive when identifying your weaknesses, as this will help you to work on them and improve yourself in the long run.

83. Use your strengths to your advantage.

Identifying and using your strengths can be a powerful tool for personal and professional development. By understanding your unique talents and abilities, you can find ways to leverage them to achieve your goals and improve your life.

One way to use your strengths to your advantage is to focus on them in your work or personal projects. For example, if you are a skilled communicator, you can use that strength to build relationships, influence others, or convey complex ideas in a clear and concise way. If you are creative, you can use that strength to develop new and innovative solutions to problems or to create original works of art.

Another way to use your strengths to your advantage is to look for opportunities to develop them further. This can include taking on new challenges or projects that allow you to use your strengths in new ways, or seeking out training or education to help you improve your skills.

Finally, it is important to recognize that everyone has weaknesses as well as strengths. By understanding your weaknesses and working to improve them, you can become a more well-rounded and effective person. This can involve seeking out feedback from others, practicing self-reflection, and working to develop new skills and abilities.

84. Work on improving your weaknesses.

Identifying your weaknesses is important, but it's equally important to work on improving them. This can be done by seeking feedback from others, researching strategies to improve in those areas, and actively practicing and incorporating new habits into your daily routine.

It's important to have patience and persistence when working on improving weaknesses, as progress may not happen overnight. Remember that everyone has areas for improvement, and focusing on them can lead to personal and professional growth.

85. Attend personal development workshops and seminars.

Personal development workshops and seminars can help you learn new skills, gain insights, and connect with like-minded individuals who are also working on self-improvement. By attending these events, you can expand your knowledge and experiences, as well as network and build relationships that can be beneficial to your personal and professional growth.

There are many workshops and seminars available on various topics, such as leadership, communication, time management, mindfulness, and more. You can find them online, through local organizations or professional associations, or by seeking out recommendations from others in your industry or community.

86. Work on developing new skills.

Continuous learning is key to personal and professional growth. Take the initiative to identify new skills you want to acquire and find ways to develop them. This could include taking classes or workshops, reading books, watching online tutorials, or finding a mentor.

It's important to choose skills that are relevant to your interests and goals, and to have a plan in place for how you will practice and apply your new knowledge. Remember to be patient and persistent in your efforts, as developing new skills can be a challenging but rewarding process.

87. Join a mastermind group to network and learn.

A mastermind group is a small group of people who come together to support each other's growth and success. They often meet regularly to share ideas, provide feedback, and hold each other accountable for achieving their goals.

Joining a mastermind group can be a great way to network with like-minded individuals and gain valuable insights and perspectives on personal and professional development. Consider researching online or asking your colleagues if they know of any mastermind groups you can join.

88. Read personal development books to gain insights and inspiration.

Reading personal development books is a great way to gain new insights and inspiration for your personal growth. There are many books out there on a variety of topics, including goal-setting, time management, communication skills, mindfulness, and more.

Some popular personal development books include "The 7 Habits of Highly Effective People" by Stephen Covey, "Atomic Habits" by James Clear, "The Power of Now" by Eckhart Tolle, and "The Miracle Morning" by Hal Elrod. Find a book that resonates with you and commit to reading it regularly to help you grow and develop as a person.

89. Practice self-reflection to improve self-awareness.

Self-reflection is an important practice to improve self-awareness, which can help you understand your thoughts, emotions, and behaviors. To practice self-reflection, set aside time to think about your experiences, actions, and decisions, and ask yourself questions such as:

- What did I do well?
- What could I have done better?
- What did I learn from this experience?
- What are my values and how do they influence my decisions?
- What are my goals and how am I working towards them?
- How do my thoughts and emotions affect my behavior?
- What are my strengths and weaknesses?

Through self-reflection, you can gain insights into yourself and develop a better understanding of who you are, what you want, and how you can improve.

90. Work on developing emotional intelligence.

Emotional intelligence (EI) refers to the ability to understand and manage one's own emotions, as well as the emotions of others. Developing emotional intelligence can lead to better relationships, improved communication, and greater overall well-being. Here are some ways to work on developing emotional intelligence:

● Practice self-awareness: Take time to reflect on your own emotions, thoughts, and behaviors. Identify patterns and triggers that may cause negative emotions, and learn to manage them effectively.

● Improve your communication skills: Learn to listen actively and empathetically, and express your thoughts and feelings in a clear and respectful way.

● Develop empathy: Put yourself in other people's shoes and try to understand their perspective and feelings.

● Manage stress effectively: Learn to recognize and manage stress in healthy ways, such as through exercise, relaxation techniques, or time management.

● Practice mindfulness: Mindfulness involves paying attention to the present moment without judgment. This can help you stay focused and calm, and improve your overall emotional well-being.

91. Use templates to save time on repetitive tasks.

Using templates can save you a lot of time on repetitive tasks, whether it's creating documents, presentations, or emails. By creating a template, you can easily reuse a format or layout that you frequently use, and customize it as needed.

This can be especially useful for businesses, as it can help maintain consistency in branding, messaging, and other important aspects of the organization's communication. There are many tools available online, such as Microsoft Office, Google Docs, Canva, and more, that offer a variety of templates for different purposes.

92. Use canned responses to respond to frequently asked questions.

Using canned responses for frequently asked questions can save you time and effort in responding to common inquiries. Canned responses are pre-written messages that can be quickly copied and pasted into an email or message.

This is especially useful for customer service or support roles, where similar questions or issues may arise frequently. By having canned responses ready, you can quickly respond to inquiries and provide consistent and helpful information to customers or clients. Just be sure to personalize the response as needed, so that it doesn't come across as too automated or impersonal.

93. Use autoresponders to manage email efficiently.

Autoresponders are a great tool to manage your email efficiently. By setting up an autoresponder, you can automatically send a pre-written email to anyone who emails you, letting them know that you have received their message and when they can expect a response.

This can save you time and help you stay organized, especially if you receive a high volume of emails. Just be sure to customize the message to fit the specific situation and provide a timeframe for when you will respond to their email.

94. Use chatbots to automate customer service.

Using chatbots to automate customer service can be an effective way to handle common questions and issues quickly and efficiently. By programming responses to common inquiries, chatbots can help free up time for human customer service representatives to focus on more complex problems.

However, it's important to ensure that the chatbot is well-designed and programmed with accurate information, and that customers have a way to reach a human representative if needed.

95. Take regular breaks to avoid burnout and maintain focus.

Taking regular breaks is an important aspect of maintaining productivity and avoiding burnout. Here are some tips for incorporating breaks into your workday:

● Schedule breaks: Set aside specific times during the day for breaks and make sure to stick to them. This could be a 15-minute break every 2 hours, for example.

● Get up and move: Use your breaks to get up from your desk and move around. Go for a quick walk, stretch, or do some light exercise to get your blood flowing and clear your mind.

● Disconnect: During your brakes, disconnect from work-related tasks and technology. Take a break from your computer, phone, and email to give your brain a rest.

● Do something enjoyable: Use your breaks to do something you enjoy. This could be reading a book, listening to music, or chatting with a coworker.

Remember, taking regular breaks is an essential part of maintaining your overall health and wellbeing, so don't be afraid to prioritize them in your daily routine.

96. Use task delegation to reduce workload.

Task delegation is a great way to reduce workload and increase efficiency. Here are some tips for effective task delegation:

● Choose the right person for the task: When delegating tasks, make sure you choose someone who has the necessary skills and experience to complete the task successfully.

● Clearly communicate expectations: Make sure you communicate your expectations clearly when delegating tasks. Explain what needs to be done, when it needs to be done, and what the desired outcome should be.

• Provide support and resources: Ensure that the person you are delegating tasks to has the necessary resources, such as tools, information, and support, to complete the task.

• Set deadlines and follow up: Set clear deadlines for the completion of the task and follow up regularly to ensure progress is being made.

• Provide feedback: Once the task is completed, provide feedback to the person who completed it. Let them know what they did well and what could be improved upon in the future.

Remember, effective task delegation is not only beneficial for you, but also helps your team members develop new skills and take on more responsibility.

97. Use collaboration tools to work efficiently with others.

• Collaboration tools can help you work efficiently with others, especially if you are working remotely or with people in different locations. These tools can help you stay connected, share documents and files, and collaborate on projects in real-time. Some popular collaboration tools include:

• Microsoft Teams: A unified communication and collaboration platform that brings together chat, video meetings, file storage, and collaboration capabilities.

• Slack: A messaging and collaboration tool that allows teams to communicate in real-time, share files, and integrate with other tools.

● Trello: A project management tool that uses boards, lists, and cards to help teams track tasks and manage projects.

● Google Drive: A cloud-based file storage and sharing platform that allows teams to collaborate on documents, spreadsheets, and presentations.

● Asana: A project management tool that helps teams track tasks, manage projects, and collaborate on work.

These tools can help you work more efficiently with others, streamline communication, and stay organized.

98. USE BATCH PROCESSING to complete similar tasks together.

Batch processing is a technique where you group together similar tasks and complete them all at once, rather than doing them sporadically throughout the day. This approach can help you save time and increase productivity by minimizing the time you spend switching between different types of tasks.

For example, if you have to respond to multiple emails, rather than responding to each email as soon as it comes in, you can batch them together and respond to all of them at once during a designated time period. This allows you to focus solely on email tasks, rather than being distracted by other tasks in between.

You can also use batch processing for tasks like making phone calls, scheduling meetings, or completing paperwork. By batching similar tasks together, you can work more efficiently and stay focused on one type of task at a time.

99. Use voice assistants to automate tasks.

Using voice assistants to automate tasks can be a great tip for improving productivity for several reasons:

● Time-saving: By using voice assistants to automate routine tasks, you can save time and focus on more important tasks. For example, you can use a voice assistant to schedule meetings, set reminders, or make phone calls while you work on other tasks.

● Multitasking: Voice assistants allow you to multitask more efficiently. You can ask your voice assistant to read out your emails while you work on a project or create a to-do list while you're cooking dinner.

● Hands-free: With a voice assistant, you can complete tasks without having to use your hands. This can be particularly helpful if you're busy doing something else, or if you have a physical disability that makes it difficult to use a keyboard or mouse.

● Accuracy: Voice assistants can help reduce errors and increase accuracy, especially for tasks that require data entry or calculations. For example, you can use a voice assistant to dictate an email, ensuring that you don't make any typing mistakes.

Overall, using voice assistants to automate tasks can be an effective way to improve productivity and make the most of your time.

100. Use outsourcing to delegate non-essential tasks.

Using outsourcing to delegate non-essential tasks can be a great tip for improving productivity for several reasons:

- Focus on essential tasks: Outsourcing non-essential tasks can free up time and allow you to focus on more important tasks. By delegating tasks such as data entry, social media management, or bookkeeping, you can concentrate on tasks that require your unique skills and expertise.

- Increased efficiency: Outsourcing tasks to someone who specializes in that area can result in increased efficiency and productivity. For example, a professional social media manager can create more engaging and effective social media posts than someone who is not an expert in that area.

- Cost-effective: Outsourcing can be cost-effective because you only pay for the work that is done, and you don't have to pay for overhead costs such as office space, equipment, or employee benefits. This can be particularly beneficial for small businesses or entrepreneurs who have limited resources.

- Scalability: Outsourcing can also help you scale your business. As your business grows, you can delegate more tasks to outsourcing partners, allowing you to focus on strategic planning and business development.

- Time zone differences: Outsourcing to different time zones can allow you to have work completed overnight, or while you're out of the office. This can result in faster turnaround times and increased productivity.

Overall, using outsourcing to delegate non-essential tasks can be an effective way to improve productivity, increase efficiency, and allow you to focus on the tasks that require your unique skills and expertise.